KAY CRAIG

REBELS:
THE SOUTHERN CRITIQUE OF CAPITALISM

sublation press

Rebels: The Southern Critique of Capitalism

First Published by Sublation Media 2026

Commissioned and Edited by Douglas Lain
Copy Editor: Konrad Jandavs

A Sublation Press Book
Published by Sublation Media LLC

Distributed by Ingramspark

www.sublationmedia.com

Print ISBN: 979-8-9988244-2-5

Edited and typeset by Polifolia

Contents

Preface

Consider the following quotations. They are all a bit verbose, a bit old-timey, but the sentiments they convey should be familiar to you. They are the common sentiments of all who oppose the capitalist system and would like to see it replaced with something better.

> Statement 1: "Neither ambition nor avarice could ever succeed in depriving nations of their liberty and property, if they did not by some artifice enlist the services of a body of men, numerically powerful. . . . And capitalists, by promising wealth to mechanicks, accumulate it for themselves, and become their masters."

> Statement 2: "In all old countries, labor is superabundant, employers less numerous than laborers; yet all the laborers must live by the wages they receive from the capitalists. The capitalist cheapens their wages; they compete with and underbid each other, for employed they must be on any terms. This war of the rich with the poor and the poor with one another, is the morality which political economy inculcates."

Statement 3: "Suppose you could divide this great country into two classes; on one side you put the wealth-producing element, on that side the wealth-consuming element. Which side would be the biggest? You know that the wealth-producing side would be. Who makes the laws largely? The wealth-consumers and not the wealth-producers. . . . Now, if you expect the wealth-consumers of this country to make, execute and construe the laws with that even and exact justice you are mighty badly mistaken."

These quotations all come from Southerners with infamous reputations for racism. The first, John Taylor of Caroline, owned 150 slaves. The second, George Fitzhugh, wrote two of the most famous defenses of slavery on the eve of the Civil War. The third, Jeff Davis, was a governor and senator from Arkansas at the height of the Jim Crow era who had been named after the leader of the Confederacy. You will meet them all, and many more, in the pages that follow. These quotations represent a phenomenon that has long fascinated and disturbed me. Many famous Southern racists, across more than a century, also held very left-wing views on economics. The criticism of capitalism was a constant theme among Southerners from the time of Jefferson until the time of George Wallace. Why was this, and what does this mean for people today who may agree with statements like those quoted above even while they denounce racism?

It is not too difficult to understand why Southerners would have a bone to pick with the capitalist system, as I will show in the chapters that follow. The North always outpaced the South in capitalist development. The South remained a region where raw materials were extracted long after the North had become home to factories and dense cities. As the great sociologist Immanuel Wallerstein has written, the "world system" is divided into privileged zones that possess sophisticated manufacturing technology and exploited zones that rely on brute labor and raw material production. The goods produced in the privileged zones trade at a premium with raw materials, meaning people in the raw material zones work more for less. Once such an inequality is established, it tends to persist, as the zones in the "center" use their wealth and power to keep the zones in the "periphery" underdeveloped. This is precisely the story of the relationship between the South and the North, both during the time of slavery and afterward. It is no wonder that, like other groups who have been on the losing end of capitalism, Southerners have formulated some sharp critiques of the system.

At one time, historians widely held the belief that a class conflict existed between the South and the North. Some of the greatest historians of the South, such as Kenneth Stampp, C. Vann Woodward, and Charles and Mary Beard, all told a version of this story. But the view that the South was ever engaged in a struggle against exploitation by the industrial North, and even against the very system of capitalism, is currently regarded as almost unthinkable within mainstream academia. Why? The reason seems to be the overwhelming focus on race among scholars of a left-wing bent. That is why today's most popular scholarly narratives about the South and slavery tend to minimize any history of conflict between the agrarian South and the industrial North. Works like Edward Baptist's *The Half Has Never Been Told: Slavery and the Making of American Capitalism* (2014) claim to show that the South was always capitalist, and that plantation owners were always on the side of Northern factory owners. That view was hugely popularized by the *New York Times'* 1619 Project, which tried to show that everything about American capitalism had its roots in slavery. These narratives are wrong, as this essay will show. The uncomfortable truth is that even as white Southerners victimized black Southerners, both were victims of exploitation by Northern capital. And, not surprisingly, the leaders of the South often recognized this exploitation and responded to it with incisive critiques of the capitalist system.

While working on this essay, I thought continually of a scene in Carson McCullers's great Southern novel *The Heart is a Lonely Hunter*. In this scene, Jake Blount, a frustrated white would-be leftist organizer, finally meets with Dr. Benedict Mady Copeland, a black doctor who shares his Marxist convictions. Tragically, although each is the only man in their small Southern town who might understand and sympathize with the other, they cannot get past the differences in their racial perspectives. The passage is worth quoting at length.

> "And the Negro," said Doctor Copeland. "To understand what is happening to us you have to—" Jake interrupted him savagely. "Who owns the South? Corporations in the North own three fourths of all the South. They say the old cow grazes all over—in

the south, the west, the north, and the east. But she's milked in just one place. Her old teats swing over just one spot when she's full. She grazes everywhere and is milked in New York. Take our cotton mills, our pulp mills, our harness factories, our mattress factories. The North owns them [...]" "Hold on!" said Doctor Copeland. "You are getting off on a tangent. And besides, you are giving no attention to the very separate question of the Negro. I cannot get a word in edgeways. We have been over all this before, but it is impossible to see the full situation without including us Negroes."

This is a variation of the persistent debate between the minority of so-called class reductionists and the much larger segment of the Left that continually reminds us of the preeminent importance of race. In the South, this debate has a peculiar edge, for the South is a region that has been heavily exploited by outside economic interests while having at the same time produced the most severe racial exploitation within the US. Obviously, these two facts are not entirely unrelated, but their relationship is not one of simple causation. The South has not been so severely exploited simply because of its racism, nor has it been so racist simply because it is so exploited. These are, to some degree, separate issues, insofar as it has been perfectly possible for various figures to effectively contest one form of abuse while leaving intact or even bolstering the other, as we shall see. For far too long, American historians treated race and slavery as secondary matters; the Dr. Copelands were savagely interrupted.

But historians have overcorrected, especially in the last two decades. Today, the Dr. Copelands are fully in ascendancy. It has become difficult to discuss any aspect of the nation's history, let alone that of the South, other than as an appendage to the matter of racial injustice.

In this essay, I will continually keep race in the picture while attempting to clarify the points where the South's two histories, of racism and of economic exploitation, touch one another. But I will err on the side of Jake Blount, because his perspective is the one that is marginalized and talked over today. I believe this perspective has value because it redirects our awareness from the simplistic dichotomy of guilt and goodness that has tended to infect all thinking about the South. This is an interpretation of Southern history that places economics at its center, that is attentive to the ways the South as a whole has been exploited and the ways its leaders have tried to resist that exploitation. If the reader finds themselves doubting the morality of such a project, I only ask them to consider who benefits from a morality that commands us to ignore the economic colonization and expropriation of a major region of the United States.

1.

Agrarian Roots

THERE IS NO DOUBT that slavery was the essential factor in forming the culture of the South. The slave system set the limits within which the Southern economy developed and the limits within which Southerners articulated their aspirations and ideals. Of course, slavery inculcated overlapping complexes about race, class, and honor that are greatly lamented today. But just as important is the fact that it kept the South almost wholly agrarian. Instead of investing in technology, slaveowners invested in slaves and land. Instead of developing infrastructure and amenities that could attract voluntary labor, they imported captives. Those who did not own slaves were left out of the money economy almost entirely, such that the local market for goods was very limited. Despite this general lack of development, the South fostered a highly prosperous class of slave-owning planters. These planters naturally came to believe that industry and cities were things that could be done without. In early America, planters took pride in their region's pastoral character.

During and after the antebellum period, the myth developed that the South had always been an "aristocratic" region. The Southern planters were sometimes called the "Cavaliers" or the "chivalry." It was supposed to be a land of short-tempered, impractical, horse-riding gentlemen who represented an unbroken continuity with the feudal nobility of England and Europe. As in much of the North, some "feudal" attitudes likely prevailed in the South during the colonial era, when inherited notions of deference and hierarchy were the norm. But by the American Revolution, the Southern intelligentsia was far more attracted to the ideal of classical figures like Cato and Cincinnatus—virtuous republican farmers—than that of the knight errant. The fact that all the "farming" was really being done by slaves was treated more as an unfortunate defect than as the defining feature of their society.

In fact, it was in the battle *against* "aristocracy" that the Southern political identity was first formed. Thomas Jefferson's Democratic-Republican movement was formed in opposition to the policies of the Federalist Party that gave America its first two presidents. Jeffersonians were especially opposed to the economic plan of Treasury Secretary Alexander Hamilton. This plan consisted of tariffs to protect infant industry, government subsidies to further support industry and infrastructure, and a national bank. "Aristocracy," to Jeffersonians, meant the cadre of elite entrepreneurs in the North who would get rich off these policies. The material reason for their opposition was simple: The South's agrarian path was already established, and the region would see little benefit from Hamilton's expensive program. Since it needed to import most of what it consumed, the South would be paying a subsidy to Northern industry via the tariff. It was in this context that Southerners began to assert their identity as a virtuous agrarian region in contrast to the North.

Thomas Jefferson's *Notes on the State of Virginia*, published in 1781, contained an apologia for the South's lack of industry and a rebuttal to the idea that federal policy should support industrialization. He wrote "the political oeconomists of Europe have established it as a principle that every state should endeavour to manufacture for itself: and this principle, like many others, we transfer to America, without calculating the difference of circumstance which should often produce a difference of result." In America, he believed, the abundance of available land made it possible for the country to avoid employing any of its citizens except in agriculture. In one of Jefferson's most famous passages, he wrote,

> Those who labour in the earth are the chosen people of God, if ever he had a chosen people, whose breasts he has made his peculiar deposit for substantial and genuine virtue. . . . Corruption of morals in the mass of cultivators is a phænomenon of which no age nor nation has furnished an example. It is the mark set on those, who not looking up to heaven, to their own soil and industry, as does the husbandman, for their subsistance, depend for it on the casualties and caprice of customers.

Of course, this statement glossed over the very large extent to which the "husbandmen" of the South depended on the "casualties and caprice of customers." Indeed, this was part of the reason they opposed tariffs: They didn't want to risk trade wars with the transatlantic purchasers of their cash crops. Still, Jefferson's contrast between the "independent" sons of the soil and the corrupt mass of workers and manufacturers was foundational for the Southern ideology in early America.

Jefferson's ideal, influential to this day as "Jeffersonianism," was that a republican society depended on a foundation of economically independent individuals. The majority of the citizenry should possess their own productive property, so as to be able to stand aloof from the manipulative influence of an employer or landlord. At the same time, they would also be free of the envy that might lead them to support measures to despoil the property of others. It was, of course, not a socialist idea; quite the opposite. But it has inspired much of the limited anticapitalist thinking that has occurred in the United States, even up to the present day. It calls for a wide distribution of property and the absence of a proletariat, conditions that the development of capitalism would inevitably destroy.

Followers of Jefferson further refined the message. John Taylor of Caroline, a planter and politician in the Virginia House of Delegates, emerged as one of the most hardline theorists of Jeffersonian Republicanism. As historian F. Thornton Miller noted, Taylor transitioned in the nineteenth century from using the term "moneyed aristocracy" with which to identify the entrepreneurial bedfellows of the Federalist party toward using "the more economic-sounding term, 'capitalists.'" Taylor identified the "restrictive system" of tariffs as a transfer of wealth from the citizenry to capitalists. In this way, it was worse than the tariff system in Russia, where at least the tariff protected government monopolies rather than private ones. "In Russia," he wrote, "the government gets the whole profit of the monopoly; here the government cannot even divide the spoils with the capitalists." He also extended Jefferson's statements about the wisdom of excluding manufacturing from the United States with a more precise critique of proletarianization. "Pauperism and crimes," he wrote, "are more frequently produced by hard labour for daily wages, than from any other source; because it usually expends the wages of today in the subsistence of today." This was the "Iron Law of Wages" first articulated by David Ricardo, which would later inspire protosocialist movements like Chartism in England. Overall, it would not be wrong to call Taylor's ideology "anticapitalist."

Neither Thomas Jefferson nor John Taylor were enthusiastic supporters of slavery, but both owned many slaves. This contradictory position was common among Old South writers and politicians. Jefferson's *Notes* condemned slavery's influence on society, asking "with what execrations should the statesman be loaded, who permitting one half the citizens thus to trample on the rights of the other, transforms those into despots, and these into enemies, destroys the morals of one part, and the amor patriæ of the other." John Taylor was less adamant but considered slavery "a misfortune to agriculture, incapable of removal, and only within reach of palliation." James Madison, John Randolph, and other leading lights of the Old South made similar statements. These men were hypocrites, no doubt, but it is worth recognizing that the South's ideological foundation was not built upon any *celebration* of slavery. What they celebrated was the agrarian, non-proletarian character of the South, which was in fact a result of slavery. However, as the pressures against the slave system mounted, this would begin to change. A new group of ideologues would emerge who thought of slavery as "a positive good."

There were two key factors that led to this change. One was the opening up, through Indian Removal, of lands in the Mississippi Valley where cotton could be grown on an industrial scale. This led slavery, formerly seen as a system destined to wither away, to become profitable and open to a new generation of Southern entrepreneurs. Slavery became something much more "modern," a speculative, booming enterprise in which fortunes could be made. At the same time, opposition to slavery grew in the North, on the part of both the growing group of highly religious radicals calling themselves abolitionists and the more common people who resented the aggression and land-greed of the new generation of Southern planters.

The question of whether the arriviste cotton planters of the mid-nineteenth century were capitalists has been perhaps the most intense scholarly controversy of the twenty-first century. Historians such as Edward Baptist, Matthew Desmond, and Sven Beckert make the case that these planters were not only capitalists but pioneers of modern capitalism. The boom in cotton fueled industrialization by providing cheap raw materials and markets for manufactured goods. Innovative financial instruments were deployed to underwrite new plantations. Baptist even argues that slaveowners invented the sorts of management techniques that would later be employed in Detroit factories.

Marxist scholars, such as Barbara Jeanne Fields, James Oakes, and Charles Post, have been the main opponents of this view. They all make the argument that slavery, even at its most modern and profit-oriented, was different from the capitalism of the North. Capitalism uses free laborers who are paid wages, can be fired, and can in theory save money and aspire to become capitalists themselves. Slave labor has none of these characteristics. There are few positive incentives in slavery, and slaves who can be neither fired nor promoted out of the condition of slavery are motivated to slow work down and resist wherever possible. Also, the cultural and financial investment in slave property means that rather than reducing the workforce to replace human labor with machinery, an essential part of capitalist development, slaveowners either acquired larger numbers of slaves or worked those they had as hard as possible. Thus, the slave economy was deprived of the gains in efficiency and profitability available in a free labor economy. Finally, the fact that slaves were not, in most cases, paid wages meant a profound concentration of discretionary income in the slave economy. A large share of the population was either outside the workforce altogether, if white, or working for no money, if black. There were exceptions, and a white urban professional class was already growing in the South on the eve of the Civil War, but it was very much in the minority. The cash was concentrated in the hands of a minority of whites, meaning that the kind of broad-based consumption that could lead to economic development did not exist. The proof of the consequences of slavery was in the obvious differences between the South and the North on the eve of the Civil War. As economic historian Peter Coclanis pointed out in his article "Tracking the Economic Divergence of the North and the South," in 1860 the South contained only 10 percent of the nation's industrial workforce, had less than 10 percent of its population in cities (compared to the Northeast's 36 percent), and had a transportation infrastructure that was built to ship out raw materials rather than to connect internal hubs of commerce and population. Ultimately, the debate over whether slavery was technically capitalist or not is one mostly of interest to academics. The fact that is more significant and harder to dispute is that slavery represented an economic interest that differed from and conflicted with industrial capitalism as it existed in the US in the mid-nineteenth century. Slavery was not the variant of capitalism that would prove most efficient for generating profits and technological innovation. Even Sven Beckert, who advocates regarding antebellum slavery as a dynamic capitalist institution, would agree with this assessment, arguing as he did in *Empire of Cotton* that slavery hindered industrialization in the areas where it was practiced, even as it facilitated industrialization elsewhere. For this reason, the South continued to lag behind the North, remaining dependent on the labor-intensive production of raw materials while the North developed a diversified and industrialized economy. The conflict between the two regions was only intensified as a result.

2.
From Necessary Evil
to Positive Good

"The Marx of the Master Class"—I recall this witty phrase provoking some uncomfortable tension in my first-year seminar in grad school. Its author was the renowned historian Richard Hofstadter, one of the bowtie-wearing superstars of America's old liberal intelligentsia. Hofstadter's work was not a big hit with my peers. The new liberal intelligentsia, in which we had come to seek our own places, is less interested in wit than Hofstadter's generation was. Hofstadter's sparkling description of the nation's foremost defender of the slave system, John C. Calhoun, was taken as offensively lighthearted.

But like all good jokes, Hofstadter's title for Calhoun contains much truth. Independently of Marx, Calhoun developed a very similar critique of the capitalist system, one intimately tied to his defense of slavery. Calhoun's anticapitalism was not incidental but fundamental to his ideology. I think that it was really the truth of Hofstadter's words that provoked us. Imbued with the testy moralism of junior academics, we didn't like hearing that someone we regarded as evil held some views very similar to our own. Hofstadter wrote that Calhoun "placed the central ideas of 'scientific' socialism in an inverted framework of moral values and produced an arresting defense of reaction, a sort of intellectual Black Mass." It is this arresting Black Mass with which this chapter, and in a sense the whole of this essay, is concerned.

John C. Calhoun of South Carolina achieved political fame as vice president to Andrew Jackson, with whom he shared a bellicose temperament and the appearance of a grizzled bird of prey. Their relationship went south quite dramatically and publicly when Calhoun anonymously published a tract declaring the right of South Carolina to ignore federal tariffs. Jackson is alleged to have said, "I have only two regrets: I didn't shoot Henry Clay and I didn't hang John C. Calhoun." Calhoun's willingness to incur the wrath of his boss, the American president, is evidence of a character that was rare at the time and basically non-existent today. He was known for being obsessive, cerebral, and humorless, with endless energy for theorizing and very little for socializing. In his most famous portrait he appears rigid, emaciated, and slightly crazed. It is a face we would now more readily associate with a brilliant mental patient than with a successful politician. Calhoun owned 200 slaves and regarded himself as a champion of the rights of minorities. The minority he championed was the outnumbered and overpowered community of Southerners. The tariff, which enriched Northern business while taxing the South, was the most galling evidence of this circumstance. In protest, Calhoun not only defended the right of states to nullify laws they disapproved of but also argued for the innate moral superiority of slavery to the system of industrial capitalism in the North.

Under capitalism, Calhoun alleged, warfare between the worker and his employer was inevitable. The employer sought to extract the maximum from the hired worker while feeling no obligation to him beyond the payment of the lowest possible wage. The worker was always inclined to strive for the overthrow of a system so hostile to his interests, rendering capitalist society inherently unstable. The slaveowner, however, had a far more harmonious relationship with the slave. All civilizations involved the extraction of wealth from labor by non-producers, Calhoun asserted in a Senate speech on abolitionism. He invited listeners to compare the "artful fiscal contrivances" by which wealth was extracted in the North to the "direct, simple, and patriarchal mode by which the labor of the African race is, among us, commanded by the European." In the South, the slaveowner treated the slave with a tender *noblesse oblige*, which was reciprocated with child-like loyalty and dependency on the part of the slave. This was a myth, as many Southerners learned to their chagrin when their slaves eagerly fled to the enemy ranks during the Civil War.

The contrast between the benevolent paternalism of the slave South and the mercenary harshness of the capitalist North was a favorite theme of Southerners in the decades before the war. The infamous "Mud-sill" speech by Calhoun's fellow South Carolina senator James Henry Hammond carried the same message. Like Calhoun, Hammond asserted that all civilization required a class "to perform the drudgery of life." "Such a class you must have," he said, "or you would not have that other class which leads progress, civilization, and refinement. It constitutes the very mud-sill of society and of political government; and you might as well attempt to build a house in the air, as attempt to build either the one or the other, except on this mud-sill." In the

South, this mud-sill was made up of black people, who in Hammond's mind were uniquely adapted to their function. He also favorably contrasted the condition of slaves with that of Northern workers, claiming,

> the difference between us is, that our slaves are hired for life and well compensated; there is no starvation, no begging, no want of employment among our people, and not too much employment either. Yours are hired by the day, not cared for, and scantily compensated, which may be proved in the most painful manner, at any hour in any street of your large towns. Why, you meet more beggars in one day, in any single street of the city of New York, than you would meet in a lifetime in the whole South.

Thus did the defense of slavery and a quite astute condemnation of Northern political economy go hand in hand.

This position was not identical to that of Jefferson. Slavery, rather than being an incidental and regrettable feature of the Southern economic system, was at the center of this novel vision. The reason for this development was the increasing criticism of slavery, coming from the North and driven by new religious ideals most prevalent in industrializing and commercial sections of the United States. What remained the same was the recognition that the South was socially and economically different from the North and that the most important feature of this difference was the South's lack of a proletariat. Calhoun et al. also retained the sense of a fundamental conflict of interest between North and South. This conflict was not based simply on the different labor systems but on the differing imperatives of industrial and agrarian economies. In Hammond's Mud-sill speech, he expounded on this difference:

> With one-fourth the present tariff, she would have a revenue with the present tariff adequate to all her wants, for the South would never go to war; she would never need an army or a navy, beyond a few garrisons on the frontiers and a few revenue cutters. It is commerce that breeds war. It is manufactures that require to be hawked about the world, and that give rise to navies and commerce. But we have nothing to do but to take off restrictions on foreign merchandise and open our ports, and the whole world will come to us to trade. They will be too glad to bring and carry us, and we never shall dream of a war. Why the South has never yet had a just cause of war except with the North. Every time she has drawn her sword it has been on the point of honor, and that point of honor has been mainly loyalty to her sister colonies and sister states, who have ever since plundered and calumniated her.

The North, because of its reliance on manufacturing, a field in which the United States had no special comparative advantage, needed to use the threat of military force to open and protect markets for its products throughout the world. The

South, meanwhile, produced cotton in greater abundance and of a higher quality than anywhere else in the world. Southern cotton sold itself and required no military power to secure its market dominance. The South didn't need the North. It could get the manufactured articles it needed anywhere while having peaceful relations with the whole world. But the North needed the South as both a captive market and a source of revenue to support the large military it required. Calhoun, too, saw the tariff as an instrument of exploitation foisted upon the South. Calhoun and Hammond denounced the modern industrial capitalist system then emerging in the North on the basis of both its labor system and the political necessities engendered by industrial production.

Some Northern reformers and radicals tied Calhoun's rhetoric to their own class-conscious political programs, and Northerners who considered themselves champions of the working class were attracted by the rhetoric. In 1844, John C. Calhoun's campaign for the Democratic presidential nomination found support among a group of left-wing Democrats in the North who were groping toward an ideology that would serve the interests of the emerging American proletariat. One might wonder how, exactly, Calhoun was supposed to help the working class. To understand the logic of left-wing Calhounism, one must understand the class politics of the antebellum era. Two distinctive features must be recognized. The first is that there was no welfare class in the nineteenth century—the rich were understood to be the primary tax-consumers. The tariff, the main source of taxation, was used to protect the profits of industrial businesses while requiring everyone else to pay a premium for goods. The second is that the nineteenth-century Left in the United States still hoped to arrest the development of a system of wage labor. Today, anyone who supports workers is generally expected to support policies that will protect and increase industrial employment. In Calhoun's time, it still seemed like the wage labor system as such could be stopped, that an economy made of self-employed proprietors could be preserved. This ideal was common among early labor reformers. For instance, the Working Men's Party of 1829, helmed by George Henry Evans, was primarily focused on securing free land in the West on which citizens could live as yeoman farmers. The goal of the emergent Left in this period was to prevent the growth of concentrated wealth and maximize opportunities for workers to become small entrepreneurs. In this context, Calhoun's efforts to disrupt the political program of the Northern capitalists, centered on tariffs, were welcomed by the Left. As the historian Arthur Schlesinger Jr. put it, Calhoun's obstruction of federal activism (through his insistince on the right of states to nullify acts like employment of the tariff) "would set up obstacles to the tendencies toward economic tyranny."

Orestes Brownson, who went from Transcendentalism to Catholicism after a highly public conversion, was one of the leading intellectual voices of the antebellum period. He was a quintessentially Northern figure; born in Stockbridge, Vermont, he made his career in the Boston and New York literary scenes. He was what was called a socialist in those days, often writing about the unjust conditions facing workers. In a famous 1844 review of Thomas Carlyle's book on Chartism, appearing in his new magazine *Brownson's Quarterly Review*, he backed Calhoun to the hilt. He especially praised Calhoun for standing against the unjust "restrictive system" of tariffs. This system was "exceedingly unjust and oppressive to the Southern section of the country" and had a lamentable "effect on the relative position of the two classes of industrials, namely, proprietors and proletaries." A subsequent article in the same issue declared that "nothing in our legislation has done more to favor the march of modern Feudalism, than the restrictive policy of Mr. Clay and his friends."

Another of Calhoun's Northern backers was the political gang-leader Mike Walsh, who Schlesinger called "the most colorful of the left-wing Calhoun leaders." Walsh was an Irish Protestant and a ferocious enemy of the Irish Catholic Tammany Hall organization that controlled New York City politics in the nineteenth century. He was one of the leaders of the working-class Protestant louts known as the Bowery B'hoys. These were the types depicted among Bill the Butcher's entourage in the film *Gangs of New York*. Like Bill the Butcher, Walsh was (paradoxically) a nativist, but he was also a spokesman for the working class who resented Tammany Hall's self-interested grip on the democratic institutions of the city. He called his followers the "Subterranean Democracy," which demanded more than a mere "change of masters" through the political process. Another characteristic statement by Walsh: "The great and fruitful source of misery in society is . . . the abject dependence of honest, willing industry upon idle and dishonest capitalists." Like Brownson, Walsh saw Calhoun as a potential champion of the "subterranean," class-conscious Democratic subculture of the Northeast.

The idea of the South as an alternative to, and enemy of, the emerging capitalist society of the North was taken to its extreme conclusion by a Virginian slaveholder named George Fitzhugh. Fitzhugh is best known for his book *Sociology for the South: Or, The Failure of a Free Society*, published on the cusp of the Civil War in 1854. While Hammond and Calhoun offered a primitive critique of capitalism that emphasized the corruptions of protectionism and that actually imagined a freer market as a route to curing the system's ills, Fitzhugh recognized the market society itself as the problem. Nor was he an agrarian. In a prototype of Immanuel Wallerstein's World-Systems Theory, he recognized that regions producing raw materials were exploited under conditions of free exchange by manufacturing regions. He went so far as to make the profoundly un-Jeffersonian statement that "the will of men can devise no better way to impoverish a country than exclusive agriculture." He wanted the South to urbanize and industrialize, to chart its own path to technological and social modernity. He was a far more precise, radical, and unromantic thinker than the more famous Southern ideologues, one whose thought seemed to have more in common with the early Marx than with Jefferson.

Fitzhugh's resemblance to Marx was not merely superficial. He characterized the system of "free trade" as tending to both "stimulate energy [and] excite invention and industry" and "[widen] the relative abilities of the weak and the strong." The rich grew richer, and the poor grew poorer, while all restraints on free, individual competition were loosed. The serfs, uprooted from the land, lived a haphazard vagabond existence before they were disciplined into being a proletariat by a "bloody code." While the abundance and sophistication of society grew, the descendants of the serfs were exploited more and more deeply. "Whilst labor-saving processes have probably lessened by one half, in the last century, the amount of work needed for comfortable support, the free laborer is compelled by capital and competition to work more than he ever did before." He also shared with Marx the contention that the reigning ideologies of each age were those of the ruling classes, fundamentally serving their interests. The foundational thinkers of liberal capitalism, like Adam Smith, belonged to the class that emerged on the top following the harsh war of all against all brought about by the abolition of feudalism. Of course, *they* saw capitalism and legal equality as progressive revolutions. For most of humanity, lacking the talents to dominate in the laissez-fair battle, these developments meant the loss of needed protection and security.

Where Fitzhugh differed from Marx, of course, was in the alternative he advocated. "Slavery," he famously wrote, "is a form, and the best form, of socialism." Slavery, as Fitzhugh defined it, was simply any system in which some subjects were prescribed roles of formal dependency upon others. The slavery of the South was one "shade" of slavery, suited to the particular racial deficiencies of blacks, in which Fitzhugh believed. But all of society would best be organized under some form of slavery, that is, with a prescribed hierarchy of obligations furnishing permanent security for the worker. Simply, most whites would be better off as slaves themselves. Labor organizations and communes were all attempts to create something for workers resembling the status of a slave, for whom sustenance was guaranteed. What Fitzhugh patently did not believe was that such a system could ever be instituted on the basis of equality. It was the false belief in equality that had in the first place justified the abandonment of the vulnerable masses by their feudal protectors. "Socialism is already slavery in all save the master. It had as well adopt that feature at once, as come to that it must to make its schemes at once humane and efficient." The difference between Fitzhugh and a left-wing socialist was that he did not believe the inescapable class conflict in society could be resolved through equality. He accepted that there were differences between people—not just racial differences but the more basic difference between the formidable few and the hapless many—that made inequality inevitable. The most humane and realistic solution was a formal contract of paternalistic obligation that bound the many to the few.

Fitzhugh, as other scholars have noted, is nearly *sui generis* in the pantheon of American thinkers. He is one of very few to break altogether with the premises of liberalism and the Enlightenment, something that until recently was only widely attempted by American Communists. Arguably, he is one of a very small number of true rightists in American intellectual life, because he fundamentally rebukes the possibility of equality or individual rights separate from government. Thus, it is almost tempting to dismiss him as a curiosity, irrelevant to the Southern tradition descended from Jefferson. Really, though, Fitzhugh was the necessary evolution of Jefferson, of the confrontation between slavery and Jefferson's ideals. Jefferson had believed that slavery was incidental to the South's agrarianism and that it would wither away, leaving an egalitarian society of yeomen. Calhoun and Hammond recognized that slavery wasn't going away, but they tried to pretend that the egalitarianism Jefferson cherished *was served* by slavery, because it freed whites from the necessity of being wage laborers. Fitzhugh finally did away with the Jeffersonian illusion altogether. He realized that the moral logic of slavery could not coexist with ideals of human equality—one must triumph over the other. Fitzhugh's view was arguably the most realistic. The South on the eve of the Civil War was not an egalitarian society. The inequality between those whites who owned slaves and those who did not was drastic. In black-belt areas, democracy essentially did not exist. The masses of whites voted with planters or they did not vote. Poor whites were in some cases publicly whipped and auctioned off as indentured servants due to their indebtedness. This social contradiction may eventually have found its resolution in some manner of more or less formal enslavement for whites. One can imagine, as Fitzhugh did, a modern, diversified South operated as a slavery-based command economy, with cities and factories built and operated by a multiracial class of peons. It is unlikely that Jeffersonian dreams could have survived forever in a South that remained committed to solving class conflict with slavery. But, of course, the South was not permitted to take this route. The war came and changed everything.

3.
The Confederate Cornerstone

No serious historian today would claim that the Southern states seceded over an abstract disagreement about "states' rights." Slavery was at the heart of both Southern society and the Confederacy's reason for existence. However, the ideology of the Confederacy was more elaborate than a simple expression of the desire to retain human property. Confederate VP Alexander Stephens' "Cornerstone Speech" is often held up as evidence that Confederate political theory began and ended with white supremacy. Stephens said, "The prevailing ideas entertained by . . . most of the leading statesmen at the time of the formation of the old constitution, were that the enslavement of the African was in violation of the laws of nature; that it was wrong in principle, socially, morally, and politically . . . Our new government is founded upon exactly the opposite idea; its foundations are laid, its cornerstone rests, upon the great truth that the negro is not equal to the white man; that slavery subordination to the superior race is his natural and normal condition."

Surely, this is irrefutable evidence that racial slavery was central to the Confederate vision. However, this statement comes near the middle of the speech, as the last in a list of ways that the Confederate Constitution differs from the Constitution of 1788. Here is the first alteration that Stephens listed, which came at the beginning of the speech: "The question of building up class interests, or fostering one branch of industry to the prejudice of another under the exercise of the revenue power, which gave us so much trouble under the old constitution, is put at rest forever under the new. We allow the imposition of no duty with a view of giving advantage to one class of persons, in any trade or business, over those of another." That is, the hated tariff—conceived in Calhounite terms as a special privilege allotted to an elite group—was done away with. This was followed by the statement that "the subject of internal improvements, under the power of Congress to regulate commerce, is put at rest under our system." No longer could one section tax others for the building of infrastructure, such as roads and canals, that benefited only them.

The idea that the Civil War was about the economic contradiction between agrarianism and industrial capitalism was once widely held by historians. This interpretation was most famously expressed in Charles and Mary Beard's *The Rise of American Civilization*, which held that the expansion of slavery into the Western territories, not slavery's mere existence, was what drove the conflict between the North and the South. But why exactly did the expansion of slavery matter? For the Beards, it was not a moral issue but a conflict between two incompatible economic interests that each sought political dominance. The war was, in a sense, about slavery, but

> "Slavery" was no simple, isolated phenomenon. In itself it was intricate and it had filaments through the whole body economic. It was a labor system, the basis

of planting, and the foundation of the southern aristocracy. That aristocracy, in turn, owing to the nature of its economic operations, resorted to public policies that were opposed to capitalism, sought to dominate the federal government, and with the help of free farmers also engaged in agriculture, did at last dominate it. In the course of that political conquest, all the plans of commerce and industry for federal protection and subvention were overborne. It took more than a finite eye to discern where slavery as an ethical question left off and economics—the struggle over the distribution of wealth—began.

The conflict between North and South was a conflict between the economic imperatives of the slave system and those of industrial capitalism.

Eric Foner's *Free Soil, Free Labor, Free Men*, published in 1970, posed a formidable challenge to the Beardian view. This book argued that Northern opposition to slavery was less a product of the manufacturing lobby than the moral outlook of small, yeoman farmers who hoped for homesteads in the West *and* believed in the inherent right of human beings to direct their own labor. Foner is a materialist like the Beards, but he had a far more sanguine view of the Republican Party and its cause. The Fonerian perspective attempts to go beyond the supposedly vulgar, follow-the-money materialism of the Beards to acknowledge the prevalence of an egalitarian moral philosophy among the Northern middle class.

The contention that the war was about a clash of ideologies runs up against the fact that the beliefs Foner attributed to the farmer base of the Republican Party were Jeffersonian beliefs; in other words, the same beliefs as those held by the Democrats. In fact, many of the rank-and-file of the Republican party were refugee Jacksonians who didn't like what they saw as large planter dominance over the Democratic Party. And their views were not meaningfully different from those of the rank-and-file Confederates, as studied by Lacy K. Ford in his book *Origins of Southern Radicalism: The South Carolina Upcountry 1800–1860*. Ford found support for the Confederacy among many white Southerners who did not own slaves, precisely because they feared that the dominance of Northern capital would lead to the loss of their yeoman independence. In other words, they held the same Jacksonian-Jeffersonian attachment to a free, landed yeomanry as small farmers in the North did. This group still made up the majority of the country's population in both the North and the South, and any political project thus needed to appeal to it. For most of the country's history before the Civil War, this group had primarily supported the Democratic-Republican Party and later the Democratic Party. What divided the sections was *the composition of their ruling classes*: large, slave-owning planters in the South and industrial capitalists in the North.

The key policies of the Republican and Democratic parties show that they *were* at least partly vehicles for these two ruling classes. In the long period of Democratic dominance of national politics prior to the election of Lincoln, Congress lowered the manufacturing tariff, reduced subsidies for shipbuilders, and prevented the restoration of a national bank. The Republican Party platform in 1860, the year Lincoln was elected, called for tariffs, financing for "river and harbor improvements," and a transcontinental railroad. After the South seceded, the Republican-dominated government rapidly began to implement this agenda, passing the high Morrill Tariff and granting entrepreneurs land and money with which to build the transcontinental railroad. The policy the Republican Party immediately began to follow was not that of the Jeffersonian yeoman but that of the crony capitalist. The Republican Party has mostly continued to follow this policy to the present day. The sectional controversy was a ruling-class controversy, in which the middle and working classes were enlisted, as they always are in such conflicts.

Why did the North, freed from the albatross of Democratic legislators by the Southern secession, go to war to stop secession? Most historians agree that Abraham Lincoln willingly provoked the attack on Fort Sumter that began the war. Most people, I think, take it for granted that "the Union had to be preserved." But why? Southern secession allowed the Northerners in Congress to push through the agenda of ambitious internal improvements that their Southern colleagues had obstructed, and it (nearly) removed from the body politic the stain of slavery with which the more cultivated Northern public was disgusted. So why didn't the North just wish good riddance to bad rubbish and leave the South alone? One historian who offered a controversial answer was Kenneth Stampp in his 1951 book, *And the War Came: The North and the Secession Crisis, 1860–1861*. By no means a conservative, Stampp was known for refuting Southern apologist accounts of slavery and Reconstruction. However, in this book, he made the case that Northern business elites pushed for war in order to preserve their monopoly on trade with the South. Southern abrogation of the tariff would have meant the loss of a huge market for Northern manufacturers, as well as the possibility that foreign goods would easily be smuggled north by way of the Confederacy. Foreign nations might also have seen an opportunity to punish the North for its protectionism by favoring trade with the South. Essentially, secession meant the loss of a captive, colonial market.

To be sure, there were substantial loyalties that motivated the lower classes of each section to support the war. In the North, the workers and small farmers wanted to preserve their chance at Western lands that would otherwise go to planters. In the South, the same class was convinced a Northern victory would mean a loss of its own yeoman freedom. But as the war went on, it became clear that in both sections, the investment in the war was not equal across classes. In 1863, the largest urban riot in American history took place in New York City, driven by outrage over the ability of the wealthy to buy their sons out of the draft. The largely Irish immigrant rioters focused much of their violence on the city's black population, which they resented for being both the object of white ruling-class sympathy and the putative cause of the war. In the South, desertion by poor whites was common. The poorest districts in the South had mostly voted against secession, as had the regions with the fewest slaves. The support by non-slaveholders that Ford observed was by no means ubiquitous. In one of the most celebrated incidents of desertion, in the same year as the Draft Riots, Mississippian Newton Knight formed a company of deserted Confederate soldiers to fight on behalf of the Union. The Civil War was, in a popular phrase of the day, "a rich man's war and a poor man's fight."

As we will see in the next chapter, the defeat of the South by the North inaugurated a period in which the colonial relation between South and North was harshly actualized. Northern victory meant the removal of obstacles for the political project of Northern capitalists, the direct acquisition of Southern property by Northerners, and the imposition of new forms of exploitation. Seen in this light, the Civil War was not a moral crusade, but a decisive blow by the rising capitalist class against their chief rival for the spoils of the young American nation. After the Civil War, the South, black and white, fell under the boot of capital as surely as any other victim of modern imperialism.

4.
Unreconstructed Rebels

Populism has always been a dirty word for America's elite. The way NPR talked about Populism in 2016 is the same way the major Northeastern newspapers talked about it in the 1890s. In the earlier era, the epithet was applied to the People's Party, a third party that swept the South and the Midwest, demanding redistributive taxes, government ownership of railroads, and radical banking reforms. Although historians have fiercely debated the character of the original Populists (were they racist? antisemitic?), most have acknowledged that they were one of the most important left-wing movements in American history. Only some have recognized the Southern context of the movement. Southern Populism was largely a reaction to defeat during the Civil War and the region's subsequent domination by Northern industrial capital.

Views of Reconstruction, the rebuilding and enforced political and social reform of the South after the Civil War, have shifted dramatically in the last hundred years. In the early twentieth century, William Archibald Dunning and his acolytes cemented the idea that Reconstruction was a period of grave injustice, in which incompetent and corrupt Republican governments of freed slaves and Northern invaders were foisted upon the South. For these historians, the "Redemption" of the South, in which federal troops withdrew and the mixed-race Republican governments were replaced with white Democratic ones, was a victory over tyranny. The Marxist historian W. E. B. Du Bois tried to change this perception with his book *Black Reconstruction* in 1935, which argued for the importance of black social and political progress in the Republican South, but his book failed to find a mainstream audience at the time. Eric Foner brought Du Bois's interpretation to wider and more sympathetic attention with his 1988 book *Reconstruction: America's Unfinished Revolution.* In the decades since Foner's book, nearly all mainstream historians have taken the line that Reconstruction was a virtuous enterprise, and that the only bad thing about it was that it stopped too soon.

But a careful reading of Du Bois's and Foner's work reveals a more complicated and less celebratory story than the one usually taught today. Both Du Bois and Foner wrote from leftist perspectives. They could not uncritically celebrate what was essentially a colonization project by the victorious Northern capitalists. Reconstruction allowed blacks a chance to participate in the governments of the South, pursue education, and build their own churches free from white supervision. While there was a coalition of sincere liberals and abolitionists who supported these developments as ends unto themselves, there was also, as Du Bois wrote, a "conscienceless" program of industrialism falsely conflated with the noble ideals of the former group. The Northern capitalists who backed Reconstruction were willing to support black voting simply in order to block Southern repudiation of debts or interference with the tariff. Once the South was sufficiently dominated by a capitalist leadership in sympathy with the political project of the Northern industrialists, the wealth of the North was willing to see black rights sacrificed for the sake of "reconciliation." This replacement of the old planter class with capitalist entrepreneurs was one of the prime achievements of Northern victory.

Historian C. Vann Woodward made this argument in its most forceful form in his book *The Origins of the New South*. Before Woodward, it was generally believed that the old Southern aristocracy, men of Calhoun's stripe, had taken the reins of power after the "defeat" of Reconstruction. Instead, Woodward showed that most of the "Democrats" who came to power after the collapse of the Republican governments in the South were former Whigs who supported many of the same measures as Republicans, including tariffs and government grants to railroad entrepreneurs. They were, essentially, a colonial elite, many with either origins in, or economic ties to, the victorious North. Subsequent works have argued that there was more continuity in the values and personnel that ruled the South before and after the war. Still, Woodward's book highlights a profound postwar transformation of the South's political economy that must be taken into account by anyone seeking to understand the region's post-Civil War history.

There were, Woodward wrote, "Some surprising naturalizations of Yankee capital into Confederate citizenship" in the Redemption period. For example, the Reconstruction government in Louisiana established a lottery corporation that quickly became one of the most profitable enterprises in the state and a source of bribery. Though Redeemers claimed to oppose corruption and the lottery, the lottery survived and flourished under the Democratic government. Its owner managed to win the endorsement of former Confederate generals P. G. T. Beauregard and Jubal A. Early, and the lottery was rebranded as a proud Southern institution. Similar cases in which Reconstruction enterprises sunk their roots into the Redeemed South abounded. Noted scalawag Joseph E. Brown joined with the Radical Republicans in Georgia during Reconstruction, being made chief justice of the Supreme Court and amassing a fortune through various industrial enterprises with the help of the government. He later became a leading Redeemer, serving as one-third of the "Bourbon Triumvirate" that controlled Georgia's politics for two decades. Even if Southern planters retained privileged positions in the New South, it was by no means the case that plantation slavery by any other name was comfortably restored. The New South was ruled by capitalists.

The dominant figure in postwar cotton agriculture was no longer the great landowner but the "furnishing merchant," a figure who was frequently Northern in origin and dated from the Reconstruction period. These were people who sold farmers, on credit, the implements needed to raise a cotton crop in return for the promise of future payment in cotton. The value of this payment greatly exceeded what the seed and implements would cost if bought outright. By design, farmers were rarely able to cancel their compounding debt to the furnishing merchant and remained perpetually obligated to him. Essentially, whether they were landowners or tenants on a planter's land, they became the employees of the furnishing merchant. The sharecropping system, in which tenants paid for land with a share of their crop, is a more widely publicized evil today. The image of disproportionately black tenants living in peasant-like fashion on the land of former slave masters fits with the idea that the slave system endured after the Civil War. But contemporary sources suggest that the furnishing merchant frequently took precedence over the landowner in their demands on the tenant's time and resources. Over time, the furnishing merchants became major landowners themselves, acquiring plantations from the fallen gentry of the pre-war South.

In his landmark 1976 study of Populism, *Democratic Promise*, Lawrence Goodwyn argued that it was principally against these men that the original Southern Populists rebelled. The first Farmers' Alliance organizations, which later formed the basis for the People's Party, were formed in order to circumvent the furnishing merchants by pooling resources. The plan was to unite small cotton farmers to secure sane terms of credit from banks on the basis of their future crops, and to use this credit to buy seed and implements at wholesale prices. They were disillusioned when banks refused to extend credit to the massive Alliance Exchange cooperative established in Dallas, which Alliancemen took to be the result of political pressure from the merchants. This episode convinced members of the Farmers' Alliance that they needed to go into politics in order to overthrow the Redeemer government that served capital.

Another problem Southern farmers faced after the war was the shortage of money itself. Confederate money was rendered worthless after the Civil War, and this meant a dire lack of circulating currency in the South. This was one of the factors that forced farmers to grow only cotton and to deal exclusively with the furnishing merchants who would accept it as money. Meanwhile, there was a movement led by Northern capitalists to contract the national supply of currency still more. During the Civil War, Lincoln had issued "Greenbacks," a fiat currency not redeemable for gold. Many Northern capitalists had used this currency to buy war bonds, which now were to be repaid with interest. While the nominal value of a bond remains fixed, its real value is determined by the buying power of money. Large bondholders therefore hoped to remove Greenbacks from circulation and replace them with gold-backed currency, which would cause deflation and increase the bonds' value relative to the prices of other goods.

The interests of the cash-strapped Southern farmers were the opposite. First, the mere ability to access currency offered a potential escape from in-kind debt peonage. Second, the more currency in circulation, the greater the inflation, the more the real value of farmers' debts would decrease relative to the cotton they sold for a living. For people struggling under the cotton lien system, Northern capitalists' demand for a return to the gold standard was thus seen as a ploy by Wall Street to enrich itself at the expense of the impoverished South. The closely related problems of currency shortage and debt were compounded by the ongoing hardship of the tariff, now higher than it had been before the Civil War. Even without its slaves, the South was still a region that produced raw material, relying on high-priced finished goods imported from the North. The class position of the South's new interracial peasantry was closely linked to its misfortune of living in a conquered province.

The People's Party, originating in the grievances of cotton farmers in the colonized South, was able to build a coalition that included all those left behind by the Republican Party's program of prosperity. The 1877 strike by workers on the heavily state-supported railroad lines owned by Jay Gould dramatized the unworkability of this program for most Americans, as did the successive economic "panics" of '73 and '93. The People's Party offered a remedy of government ownership of industries, shortened working days, free trade, and loose credit. The Populists came their closest to national power in the election of 1896, which pitted William Jennings Bryan against William McKinley. Bryan ran on a blended Populist-Democratic ticket, focusing on the unifying issue of monetizing silver in order to expand the currency supply and ease credit. McKinley stood for the Republican program of a strict gold standard and high tariffs. McKinley won and Bryan lost, consolidating the victory of industrial capital over agriculturalists and workers.

Among the circumstances that have tarnished the name of Populism is the way its twilight bled into the dawn of Jim Crow. Tom Watson, the leader of Populism in Georgia and Bryan's VP in the 1896 election, had been a strong advocate of interracial unity for the South's poor agricultural class. He made many of the sorts of statements that left-wing historians most adore, such as, "You are kept apart that you may be separately fleeced of your earnings. You are made to hate each other because upon that hatred is rested the keystone of the arch of financial despotism which enslaves you both." This idea was fundamental to Populism, which some historians have seen as the greatest force for racial harmony in the South before the Civil Rights Movement. The white ex-Confederate soldier R. M. Humphrey founded the Colored Farmers' National Alliance and Cooperative Union in Texas in 1886, and at the first meeting of the Texas People's Party in 1891, a precursor to the national party, two black executive committee leaders were elected. One of these, John B. Rayner, would become one of the best-known Populist stump speakers in Texas. But by the first decade of the twentieth century, Watson had changed his tune. In 1904, he said he would throw his support behind a candidate for governor who would write the exclusion of the black vote into the constitution of Georgia.

The justification for supporting the measure was that the black vote divided the Southern poor. Blacks could be swayed to vote with the white elite out of the fear of poor whites, while poor whites could simultaneously be browbeaten into opposing Populist reform through the threat that any radical change would bring "Negro domination." This was the pattern of the Redeemer elite's response to Populism. They rallied the black vote against the third party while paradoxically spreading the message that a Populist victory would mean the persecution of whites, the sullying of white women, and so on. If building interracial unity was the ideal solution to this conundrum, removing black people from politics was the expedient one.

In one reading, the defeat of Populism and the advent of Jim Crow represented the end of effective class consciousness in the South. Racial solidarity had established a false consciousness that left the region's white workers benighted collaborators in their own exploitation. But the story is more complicated and more uncomfortable than this. The fact is that, as we shall see, a significant awareness of economic exploitation persisted among Southerners who were also racist. It may even be argued that the "settling" of the racial issue through segregation and the exclusion of black voting did have some of the effect that Watson hoped for. More whites probably felt free to assert their class interests in the absence of a black "threat." The next chapter will show the persistence of a Populist element in the lily-white Southern Democratic party long after the establishment of Jim Crow.

5.
Stump Speakers

EVEN AS IT DEFEATED the challenge of Populism, the Southern Democratic party was also remade by Populism. If white solidarity were to be maintained, the party could not simply dismiss the concerns that drove the People's Party's successes. Additionally, a number of former Populists reentered the party with the death of the third-party movement, influencing its direction. The effect was compounded by the implementation of the Populist demand for a direct primary in most Southern states in the 1890s and 1900s, which meant that the nominating process was thrown open to qualified (white and not dirt-poor) voters rather than being controlled by party machines. This led to an influx of colorful, demagogic Southern politicians who combined race-baiting with redistributive economics. Historians have called these politicians the Southern Progressives, a term that might engender some confusion among readers accustomed to identifying Progressivism with the likes of Alexandria Ocasio-Cortez.

Perhaps the two best-known politicians to exemplify the influence of Populism on the Jim Crow era were James K. Vardaman of Mississippi and "Pitchfork" Benjamin Tillman of South Carolina, each of whom served as both governor and senator of their respective state. Both were vicious Southern rednecks straight out of central casting. Vardaman wore a ten-gallon hat over his shaggy hair and proclaimed that he would see "every Negro [in Mississippi] lynched . . . to maintain white supremacy." Glowering from his one good eye, Tillman crowed over his night-riding Reconstruction escapades on the Senate floor. But both men were reformers on economic issues. Vardaman fought against convict leasing, corporate land ownership, and regressive taxation. Tillman won railroad regulation and a law blocking corporate donations to candidates. Of course, both opposed the tariff.

Other Southern reformers of this era include Jeff Davis of Arkansas, termed "Karl Marx for Hillbillies" by one newspaper, Hoke Smith of Georgia, James Comer of Alabama, and Charles B. Aycock of North Carolina. All were ardent white supremacists, all served as governors and then as senators, and all challenged the capitalist interests in their states, especially the railroads. Smith lowered maximum working hours in the textile industry, increased funding to public schools, increased the power of the Railroad Commission, and ended convict leasing. At the urging of his ally Tom Watson, he also passed the Grandfather Clause in Georgia to disenfranchise voters. His race-baiting on the gubernatorial campaign trail helped incite the Atlanta Race Riot. Jeff Davis, the most colorful and politically ineffectual of the group, dedicated himself, not very successfully, to ending convict leasing and breaking up "trusts" in his state. He was also an ultra-racist, stating that Southerners had "come to a parting of the ways with the Negro." James Comer had, like Tillman, been an active participant in Reconstruction-era violence in his state—with his brother he led the Eufala massacre in 1874 to stop blacks from voting. He was less of an all-around Progressive on economic matters; for example, he supported child labor. But he led the fight to cut railroad rates and inhibit lobbying by the railroad companies. Aycock was also the perpetrator of a racial massacre, leading the overthrow of Wilmington's government in 1898. As governor he was primarily known for raising taxes to support public education and for going after railroads.

By the way, it is interesting to note that convict leasing was such a frequent target for some racist politicians, such as Vardaman, Davis, and Smith (Aycock instead expanded it). Today, it is common to hear talk about convict leasing being a continuation of slavery and a reflection of the South's persistent white supremacist system, along the lines presented in the film *Thirteenth*. Convict leasing, in which disproportionately black prisoners were leased to private companies by state governments, emerged in the context of Reconstruction. The first convict leasing program after the Civil War was instituted by the Union general Thomas Ruger in Georgia for work on the Georgia and Alabama Railroad. One of the largest "employers" of convict labor in the South was the Tennessee Coal, Iron and Railroad Company (TCI). This raw-material-extraction company, one of the largest in the postwar South, was helmed in the '80s and '90s by COO Hiram Bond, a New York investor who won a federal judgeship in Virginia during Radical Reconstruction and was noted for his racial liberalism. He oversaw the company's move from Tennessee to Alabama in 1895 due to the latter state's greater favorability toward convict leasing. When the company was acquired by Pittsburgh-based US Steel in 1907, it increased its exploitation of convicts further, with 60 convict laborers dying in its first year of ownership. It was the South's new rulers, not its defeated plantation elite, who took the lead in developing the resource of imprisoned workers.

As the history of the TCI indicates, the rabble-rousing of the Progressives did not effectively arrest the parceling up of the South's human and natural resources among capitalists. The company, along with a handful of other industrial firms known as the "Big Mules," effectively controlled the government of Alabama's capital city of Birmingham into the 1940s. The city used the "commission" system of government, in which a small number of expert managers controlled the entire administration of Birmingham without the interference of a legislature. These managers, which included Public Safety Commissioner Bull Connor, were firm friends of the company and its allies. Birmingham was far from the only such town. The city of Kingsport, Tennessee was purchased outright by New York bankers in the 1910s and developed as an industrial center. The attractions were its plentiful mineral deposits and its ductile, unlettered workforce. Nearly all the enterprises that would be established within the city ended up extracting and refining local raw materials. Kingsport was run by a "city manager" appointed directly by the Kingsport Improvement Corporation. The city was both exploitative and paternalist, providing insurance and annual picnics for all its worker-residents. In Memphis, the state's capital, "two thirds of the business and nearly all of the public utilities . . . were owned by Northerners during the progressive era," according to historian Charles Ayers. In 1938, the controversial *Report on the Economic Conditions of the South* would confirm that "almost all of the region's public utilities, major railroad systems, natural gas, iron ore, coal, limestone, bauxite, zinc, and sulphur deposits, as well as its cotton mills, were owned and controlled by Northern capital." In that sense, the Populist movement was certainly a material failure in the South, despite its enduring political influence.

The kind of partial, race-haunted class consciousness evinced by the left wing of the Southern Democrats during the Progressive Era would remain a factor in American politics until the late twentieth century. Its achievements may have been limited, but its mere existence challenges the view of a static South that clung to reactionary nostalgia for the plantation regime. The militant Southern politics of the early twentieth century represented a challenge to the dominion of capital, not just in the South but nationwide. The 1896 election may have seemed to seal the fate of the South and confirm the dominance of Northeastern capitalists over American politics. But in 1912, the 1896 consensus was dramatically unsettled with the election of the first Southern president since the Civil War and one of the most controversial in American history: Thomas Woodrow Wilson.

6.
Written in Lightning
The Southern Presidency of Woodrow Wilson

Woodrow Wilson made a number of monumental and extremely controversial decisions during his presidency, but it is a relatively small one that defines his legacy for many of his contemporary critics. That is his decision to screen D. W. Griffith's film *The Birth of a Nation* at the White House. Based on the novels of Thomas Dixon, a childhood friend of Wilson's, it was a polemical depiction of the South's persecution during Reconstruction and the heroic resistance staged by the Ku Klux Klan. The intertitles contained words drawn from Woodrow Wilson's own book *A History of the American People,* in which Wilson lamented "the veritable overthrow of civilization in the South" that proceeded from Reconstruction. Wilson was raised in Virginia, and writers have frequently taken his association with the film as representative of his administration's Southern, white supremacist character. In fact, Wilson probably did not know the subject of the film when he agreed to the screening, and it is doubtful that he ever uttered the assessment attributed to him: "It is like history written in lightning, and the most terrible thing is that it is all true."

Nevertheless, the story persists because there was a true and profound entanglement between his presidency and the backlash against Reconstruction. Wilson's administration brought the white supremacist Progressivism of the early twentieth-century

South to a position of national dominance. His most infamous act was permitting his cabinet to segregate the federal civil service, reversing the progress of a growing black middle class composed of government employees. As we have seen, however, there was no necessary contradiction between racism and Progressivism. In the post-Populist South, a reformist economic position that addressed Southern grievances against Northern capital coincided with pandering to Southern racial prejudice. It was both racial retrenchment *and* economic reform that defined the reaction against Reconstruction and the domination of the crony-capitalist Republican Party. Wilson was a relatively moderate, electable embodiment of this backlash.

The program Wilson campaigned on, which he called "The New Freedom," bore a marked resemblance to the ideas that had united labor and Southern Democrats in the Calhoun era. The New Freedom centered on revoking the special privileges of Northeastern capital. In a text outlining his agenda, he wrote, "Our government has been for the past few years under the control of heads of great allied corporations with special interests. It has not controlled these interests and assigned them a proper place in the whole system of business; it has submitted itself to their control. As a result, there have grown up vicious systems and schemes of governmental favoritism (the most obvious being the extravagant tariff)." Such statements would by no means have been out of place during the antebellum period.

The New Freedom was framed in explicit contrast to the program of Wilson's Northern Progressive rival, Teddy Roosevelt, whose "New Nationalism" called for an acceptance of big corporations provided they submitted to a close relationship with the government. Though Wilson and Roosevelt were both influenced by the Progressive movement, the programs they touted were distinctly Jeffersonian and Hamiltonian, respectively. Wilson rejected the idea that corporations should be a permanent part of American life or enjoy a symbiotic relationship with government. To Wilson, it was intolerable that combinations of capital had achieved such ascendancy in the country that new entrants were hopelessly excluded. He promised to craft "a body of laws which will look after the men who are on the make rather than the men who are already made." This statement must be understood in the context of a country in which Northeastern-centric corporate business and finance, with the cooperation of the Republican Party, seemed to have achieved near-total dominance over American society. Wilson spoke, in part, for a Southern agrarian bloc still hoping to contest this dominance by new means.

Wilson's election on this platform, as the first Southern president after the Civil War, was a national repudiation of the Gilded Age and the dominance of the pro-business Republican Party. One of his first acts in office was to significantly reduce the tariff rates via the Underwood Tariff of 1913. He replaced the missing tariff revenue by implementing a progressive federal income tax, one of the measures the Populists had advocated for. The next year, he led the creation of the Federal Trade Commission. The commission building was fronted by two allegorical statues depicting muscular men wrestling the wild horses of the market into submission. It would quickly take on a role that more closely reflected the New Nationalism than the Jeffersonian rhetoric of New Freedom. That is, it primarily investigated and negotiated with corporations that were behaving antisocially, rather than breaking them up. Nonetheless, it represented a substantial reversal from the Gilded Age period in which the function of the interventionist state was primarily to abet capitalists' accrual of wealth.

While in office, Wilson would be pushed further to the left by the more radical Southerners in the legislative branch. When Wilson assumed the presidency, the Democratic party in Congress was dominated by Southerners, among whom were post-Populist hardliners like Vardaman and Tillman. According to Wilson biographer Arthur S. Link, it was the influence of this faction that led Wilson to segregate the civil service. The group pushed for a Federal Reserve system controlled by the government rather than banks, with provisions for agricultural credit, and it stood behind the various acts providing agricultural credit and marketing services to farmers, such as the Rural Credits Act and the Lever Warehouse Act. These measures resembled the Populist subtreasury plan, giving farmers the means to access credit and sell their crops using government services rather than exploitative local agents. The Southern white supremacists made their influence felt through such measures just as much as through racism.

The Southerners in Congress also shaped the war policy of the United States in a left-wing direction. To the Populist-influenced congressmen of the West and South, American entry into World War I served the interests of Northeastern arms manufacturers and Wall Street bankers with investments in England and France. Southerners were leading opponents of "preparedness" and were committed to making Northeastern capital bear the brunt of the costs of war. The Southern-controlled Ways and Means Committee was behind the Wilson-backed special tax on profits made by corporations during the war. This was recognized as a sectional measure by outraged Republicans, such as Representative Joseph Fordney, who said that "78 percent of all corporation and income taxes in 1916 were paid by ten Northern, mid-Northern, and Western states," and that "the Administration received its strongest support from ten States which pay but one-fifth of the taxes."

Wilson was by no means a radical president, but he was arguably the furthest to the left on economic matters up to that time. His domestic economic program was one of reform and redistribution. In this pursuit, Wilson was inspired by a Southern vision and Southern grievances. The longstanding Southern resentment of the political power held by Northeastern capital was behind his choice to replace one system of "governmental favoritism," that of the postbellum Republican Party, with another, one geared toward the interests of Southern farmers. There was, in his approach, a continuity with Calhoun and Hammond. The link was not ideological but structural. Wilson's agenda, like theirs, was based on a recognition that the economic interests of the North and the South diverged, that the South was structurally disadvantaged, and that only a shift in the balance of political power between North and South could remedy their imbalance in economic power. Wilson's policies anticipated the more total revolution in the relationship between government and society that came with the New Deal. As much as the New Freedom, the New Deal would be shaped by Southern interests.

7.
Revolution in Government
The New Deal

No fact more clearly scuttles the popular view of the South as a "conservative" region than the overwhelming Southern support for Franklin D. Roosevelt's New Deal. Of course, the Left is used to thinking of the New Deal as a set of bourgeois reforms intended to stem popular enthusiasm for real revolution. Still, it's worth remembering that the New Deal altered the relations between the state and the market to an extent previously unimaginable. Of course, the state had not been accustomed to staying out of the market prior to the New Deal. The postwar Republican Party was highly activist, albeit on behalf of corporations. Wilson and the other Progressive presidents had passed a number of public-spirited regulatory measures. But the ethos of the New Deal was entirely different from either of these. Fundamentally, it was a program of state supremacy. The state would be the final provider of sustenance and the final arbiter of the public good. With the chary view of human freedom it implied, one can see in the New Deal a faint echo of the theories of Fitzhugh.

The historian most responsible for restoring to public attention the critical role of the South in the New Deal is Ira Katznelson, with his 2013 book *Fear Itself: The New Deal and the Origins of Our Time*. Katznelson stated that the South, as demonstrated by the Wilson presidency, was perfectly willing to seek the frontiers of activist government provided segregation went untouched. He quantitatively demonstrated the solid support that Southern Democrats in Congress had for the New Deal in its initial phases. The South, of course, had good reason for supporting government measures to end poverty and develop deprived areas of the country. For the South, the Depression was really nothing new, as the region had been depressed since the Civil War. In the minds of many Southerners, the New Deal "offered the South the chance to escape its colonized status while keeping its racial order safe." The fact that congressional support for the New Deal was disproportionately Southern meant that the New Deal disproportionately served the South. Where Populism had failed, the New Deal would succeed in partially stemming and reversing the flow of extraction from South to North.

One of the most significant boons the New Deal conferred on the South was the Tennessee Valley Authority. The legislation was coauthored by John E. Rankin of Mississippi, one of the most famous racists in Congress and an ardent FDR supporter (Rankin was one of the few to embrace Roosevelt's scheme to pack the Supreme Court). The TVA was founded to develop hydroelectric power in the Tennessee River Basin, covering all of Tennessee and parts of Mississippi, Kentucky, Alabama, and Georgia. The tax-funded hydroelectric dams created under the aegis of the TVA provided both employment for communities that had little industry besides tenant farming and cheap power for communities that had mostly gone without electricity. It was a rebuke to the historic dependence of the South on Northern-owned utility companies. The consequences of the TVA for the areas it served cannot be overstated. In addition to hydroelectric dams, the TVA built roads, schools, and canals. The projects both provided jobs to the area and, due to the availability of cheap power and transportation infrastructure, incentivized the relocation of sophisticated manufacturing industries to the South. A study by Patrick Kline and Enrico Moretti of the UC Berkeley economics department shows that the TVA brought 20 billion dollars of federal money to the South, mostly in the 1940s and '50s, or roughly 750 federal dollars per year to each household in the TVA region. From 1940 to 1960, the TVA region saw a rate of employment growth in both agriculture and manufacturing that was more than 10 percentage points greater than that in the rest of the country. Just as important for understanding the significance of the TVA is that it had no net positive impact for the country as a whole. It was a true wealth transfer. As Kline and Moretti write, "We estimate that the spillovers in the TVA region were fully offset by the losses in the rest of the country." The TVA brought money and manufacturing from North to South at federal command.

The Agricultural Adjustment Act was another measure especially welcomed by the South. In simple terms, the AAA put a floor under the prices of crops, including cotton. It incentivized the reduction of acreage in order to tighten supply and increase prices. In the case of cotton, this meant planters received a payment for every acre they withdrew from production; in practice, this amounted to a payment substantially greater than the one they would have received for producing. As historian Donald H. Grubbs writes, "One candid farmer avowed that the South was out 'to get the Civil War debt back' and then some." This attitude was widespread among cotton planters who "became even more dedicated Democrats than before." For sharecroppers, disproportionately black, the policy was unfortunate. Landowners failed to share the income with their tenants as they were supposed to and, newly cash-rich, now found it possible to replace tenants with wage labor and new farming equipment. The AAA and its successor farm programs hastened the modernization of Southern cotton farming for the good of landowners and the ill of tenants. With the AAA, the declasse planters took a leap forward into prosperity.

Roosevelt was willing to permit substantial racism in the administration of New Deal programs in order to reward Southern enthusiasm for his agenda. Ira Katznelson writes that the main methods employed to accommodate Jim Crow in New Deal legislation were "a decentralization of responsibility that placed administrative discretion in the hands of state and local officials whenever possible, a recognition in law of regional differentials in wage levels, and the exclusion of maids and farmworkers—fully two-thirds of southern black employees—from key New Deal programs." This exclusion applied, for example, to Social Security and the National Industrial Relations Act. On a national level, the white South backed a statist redistribution of wealth to rectify the economic injustice inflicted on its region. But internally, it wanted to maintain the hyperexploitation of blacks. One quote selected by Katznelson is telling: "As one commentator put the point in referring to Senate Majority Leader Joseph Robinson of Arkansas, 'So long as they [New Dealers] fought the money power and the big industries—so long as they were pro-farmer and did not stir up the niggers—he was with them.'"

Of all the Southern New Dealers, the one who perhaps best represented this seemingly hypocritical position was Theodore Bilbo, the "redneck liberal." Bilbo is best remembered today for writing a book titled *Take Your Choice: Separation or Mongrelization.* As can be discerned from its title, the book was a strident defense of segregation as a bulwark against race-mixing. He was also a left-wing New Dealer and one of the most loyal backers of Roosevelt. Bilbo was the political mentee of James K. Vardaman and carried forward the very same tradition of racist Progressivism that Vardaman embodied. Like John E. Rankin, he supported Roosevelt in his unpopular battle with the Supreme Court. As his biographer Chester Morgan writes, "The 'money power,' Bilbo declared, had been using the Republican Party to pack the Supreme Court since Lincoln's day. They had stocked it and the lower courts with a galaxy of corporation lawyers who 'by their decisions . . . have glorified property rights by sacrificing human rights.'" Bilbo backed Roosevelt's minimum wage law when other Southern politicians worried it would undercut the South's competitive advantages. His support for the measure was a reflection of his hatred for the Mississippi lumber mills that urged him to oppose it. The archetypal racist Bilbo followed Roosevelt as far left as he went, continuing in the footsteps of Vardaman.

It is informative to look at who in the South opposed the New Deal from the outset. The core pockets of resistance to the early New Deal in the South were in cities, specifically those cities controlled by business interests. Birmingham, Alabama, for example, where the Big Mules held sway, was an anti-Roosevelt stronghold. The CEO of Tennessee Coal, Iron and Railroad, Charles DeBardeleben, along with the CEOs of Republic Steel and Woodward Iron financed an anti-New Deal magazine called *Alabama* and "bankrolled a faction of the Democratic party headed by state senator James Simpson, a corporation lawyer with well-known antilabor and anti-New Deal sympathies." It was the business elite that Southern rabble-rousers like Bilbo and Vardaman had long opposed that were most likely to be anti-New Dealers in the South. More broadly based Southern opposition to the Roosevelt administration would not emerge until later, in reaction to growing civil rights pressure within the Democratic Party in the context of World War II and the CIO's interracial organizing campaigns. Fear of the latter would lead the South to strongly support the Taft-Hartley "Right to Work" bill in 1947. Nevertheless, most of the formerly unimaginable innovations in government that coincided with the New Deal's greatest period of momentum occurred with the backing of most Southern politicians and the opposition of industrial interests.

The New Deal transformed the South. While the massive investment of federal money in the region did not nearly eliminate the profound economic gap between the South and the North, it did bring the South into the modern world. The abject agrarian poverty and indebtedness of the postbellum South was replaced by an economic situation that more nearly approached "American" standards. The New Deal was, in a sense, the culmination and fulfillment of the political project advanced by the Populists and carried forward by the Progressives. Following

World War II, the Civil Rights Movement launched an assault on Southern peculiarity that, coupled with its gains in prosperity, made the region more like the rest of the country. Still, even if the Southern crusade against Northern capital had lost some of its motive force, the distinctive political consciousness of the South did not die out altogether.

8.

George Wallace
The Last Rebel

No course or documentary about the Civil Rights Movement is complete without footage of Alabama Governor George Wallace proclaiming, "Segregation today, segregation tomorrow, segregation forever!" Alongside Birmingham Public Safety Commissioner Bull Connor, Wallace is one of the iconic embodiments of white Southern bigotry making its last stand in the 1960s. In 2022, former Wallace ally Joe Biden asked his Atlanta audience, "Do you want to be on the side of Dr. King or George Wallace? Do you want to be on the side of John Lewis or Bull Connor? Do you want to be on the side of Abraham Lincoln or Jefferson Davis?" This rhetorical question, which predictably inflamed Republican outrage, captures the popular understanding of George Wallace as the final product of the lineage of Southern villainy. (Actually, it may be optimistic to refer to a popular understanding of George Wallace, given the number of articles that appeared following Biden's comments, offering to explain who George Wallace, Bull Connor, and indeed Jefferson Davis were.)

Wallace certainly does belong to a long Southern legacy. He was a segregationist, a critic of concentrated wealth, and an advocate of redistribution. His was the legacy of the Southern New Dealer, the demagogic Progressive Democrat, the Populist. In his

1968 run for president, he repeated a phenomenon that hadn't been seen since Calhoun—a racist Southern politician building a movement on the grievances of the Northern industrial working class. Wallace was the last major politician from the South to evince the distinct legacy of Southern class consciousness with which this essay is concerned. Ideologically, he had travelled a long distance from Taylor, Calhoun, and Hammond. Certainly, there was nothing anti-industrial in his outreach to steel and auto workers in Detroit and Pennsylvania. What he had in common with them, and with his more immediate predecessors, was a willingness to attack concentrated wealth and a belief that that wealth was frequently amassed through the exploitation of the South. After Wallace, this type largely vanished from American political life, partly due to the success of the Republican Party in building a culturally conservative, pro-business coalition that included the South. Wallace's place in American history is more complicated than that of the last unreconstructed racist leader. Wallace was the last major representative of an independent political tradition centered on a distinctive class consciousness.

Wallace was governor of Alabama during some of the most famous and infamous events of the Civil Rights Movement. The protests and riots in Birmingham, immortalized with images of firemen turning high-pressure hoses on children, the beating of protestors crossing the Edmund Pettus Bridge from Selma to Montgomery, and the Birmingham church bombing that killed Addie Mae Collins, Cynthia Wesley, Carole Robertson, and Carol Denise McNair all happened while Wallace was governor. Wallace also made headlines by standing in the doorway of the

University of Alabama to protest its integration by federal troops. If anyone was the face of what the Civil Rights Movement was fighting against, it was Wallace.

Wallace began his career on the left of Alabama politics. He rose through the ranks in the 1930s and '40s, serving as an assistant district attorney, a state representative, and a judge. He was known as a sometime ally of Alabama's New Dealer governor Big Jim Folsom, a man known for taking on the "Alabama Big Mules," the industrial interests who opposed New Deal policy and controlled the government of Birmingham. As governor, Wallace followed the Southern Progressive tradition. He introduced free textbooks, doubled spending on education and healthcare, and raised the old-age pension. His approach catered to the economic have-nots of his state, a legacy inherited from his forebearers. He also took a hard stance against integration. He is famously alleged to have said, after his failed gubernatorial bid in 1958, that he had lost due to being "out-segged" or "out-niggered" by his opponent and that he would not make the same mistake again. For his 1962 campaign, he hired the Klansman Asa Carter as his speechwriter. It was Carter who drafted the famous "today, tomorrow, forever" line. Wallace's redistributive policies nonetheless benefited black and white Alabamians alike. He belonged to the last generation of Southern politicians who would cleave to this position, so contradictory in terms of today's politics.

Wallace's hick Progressivism was increasingly out-of-date in the 1960s. The South was undergoing profound economic and social changes in the postwar era. The New Deal's southward redistribution of investment contributed to the "Sunbelt" boom of Southern development. A new wave of Northern corporate investment followed the New Deal. The South's urban, suburban, and educated populations boomed during this period. The lessening of the South's regional distinctiveness meant a lessening of solidarity among its white denizens. Some prospered in the New South, and they saw the prospect of further prosperity if the South were to abandon its ferocious resistance to integration, so discouraging to investors. The growing urban and suburban middle class of the South acquiesced to integration and considered a figure like Wallace an embarrassment. The year after Wallace's most infamous speech, the 1964 Civil Rights Act passed, followed the next year by the Voting Rights Act that demolished the fence around the lily-white Democratic Party, changing completely the landscape of electoral politics. In this New South, Wallace was an anachronism, but he would not fade away quietly.

In 1968, Wallace brought his case to the nation, running for president on the American Independent Party ticket. His campaign is best remembered for his invective against hippy protestors, such as his promise to run over any "anarchist" who laid down in front of his vehicle. His run was characterized by observers at the end of the century as a foreshadowing of the Reagan Democrat coalition that has become so important in American politics, most recently in electing Trump. His core of support outside the South was working-class "white ethnics" in industrial cities. Wallace acknowledged his fanbase with the quip, "I speak fluent Polish." These were erstwhile New Deal voters who felt threatened by campus radicals, crime, and black militancy. Wallace foregrounded "the working man" in his campaign, touting his support among the union rank-and-file in Alabama and pledging increases to Social Security and funding for trade schools. At the same time, he harped incessantly on "law and order" and the local control of schools, issues with an obvious racial implication. In essence, he ran on the promise of exporting the old Southern Progressive formula to the rest of the nation.

Wallace was the bane of hippies, but he was also disliked by the emerging conservative movement. In 1968, he appeared on *Firing Line*, the television show of William F. Buckley, the intellectual leader of the conservatives. Buckley was adamant that Wallace had no place on the Right. Once, Buckley apparently referred to Wallace as a "Country-and-Western Marxist" due to his affinity for social spending. In his *Firing Line* appearance, Wallace first clashed with Buckley over the latter's citation of a poll of "200 prominent conservatives" that showed "surprising animosity to Wallace." When asked to name one prominent conservative outside the South who supported him, Wallace responded, "107,283 folks signed a petition for me. Those were steelworkers … I go out to the masses of the people with the message that I have, and I don't know any prominent conservatives." Wallace was clear that his brand of politics did not fit into the emerging conservative fusion. His Alabamian Progressivism might have appeared reactionary to people on the activist Left, but it was an entirely different movement than the conservative movement that centered parsimonious social spending, hawkish foreign policy, and Christian sexual mores.

Buckley understood the essence of Wallace's politics astutely. When asked by the moderator why conservatives opposed Wallace, he said, "They find that his background is that of a New Dealer, a person who is intensely concerned to multiply the functions of the state." He cited Wallace's record of heavy spending on hospitals and pensions in Alabama. He recognized Wallace as a "kind of Democrat" in the South who had "enormous enthusiasm" for federal spending and intervention except where it interfered with segregation. This was an accurate summation of the tradition to which Wallace belonged, a tradition that was indeed distinct from conservatism of any kind. Wallace acknowledged as much, stating that "no conservative in this country who comes out against looking after destitute elderly people ought to be elected to anything."

From that point, the conversation turned to a historical defense by Wallace of his "type of Democrat." Southerners had embraced the New Deal as a means to rise "from the bottom of the economic ladder." "But, of course," Wallace proceeded in a sharp, accusatory drawl, Buckley hasn't "told why the people of the South were on the bottom rung." Buckley's response: "It's irrelevant." Wallace disagreed. He went on to list the full record of Southern grievances against the North from the Civil War's end, from carpetbag rule, to freight discrimination, to the war debt. When Buckley suggested that these were the consequences of the South having started the Civil War, any hope of an amicable interview vanished. The interview is a fascinating relic of a particular moment in American politics, a moment when a dying breed of Southern politics made its last bid for national influence. Wallace's '68 campaign won him four Southern states and nearly 15 percent of the national vote. But it was the conservatism that Buckley represented that would go on to determine the South's future.

A Republican Party guided by Buckley's ideas successfully conquered the white South, tentatively at first with the campaigns of Goldwater and Nixon, and then in a landslide with Reagan. There is some debate over why and how this happened. What seems likely is that the rising bloc of prosperous and semi-prosperous white Southerners supported the party for the same reasons as their peers across the country: the Republican Party remained the party of business, just as it was in the days of Ulysses S. Grant. Meanwhile, with black voting back on the table, poorer whites felt newly insecure, less willing to support programs of social welfare that might also aid in the social uplift, and possible dominance, of blacks. The state, with which they had such a positive relationship during the New Deal, now appeared hostile. They were willing to submit to a program of "anti-government" conservatism that promised to protect their freedom from activist intrusion and expropriation. As a result, the South is once again dominated by a Republican Party that serves the interests of capital, still overwhelmingly concentrated outside the South. The South has once more been spuriously "Redeemed."

But not everyone was willing to swallow this bitter medicine. George Wallace ran for president twice more, in 1972 and 1976. He never recaptured the success of his '68 run. In 1972 he was shot by a would-be assassin and paralyzed from the waist down. Though he had long claimed to repudiate racism, the shooting seemed to bring about a more genuine change of heart. He disavowed his past support for segregation and underwent a conversion to evangelical Christianity. In 1982 he ran for governor of Alabama one last time and won with a large majority of the black vote. On his final campaign trail, the old battler declared, "We'll talk about people who are unemployed and hungry and about Republicans who only have to worry about who will mow their beachfront lawns."

Conclusion

The South today resembles the North far more than it used to, probably more than it ever has in the history of the country. Still, there are differences too great to ignore, even as many would like to ignore them. One in five Southern counties has had a poverty rate above 20 percent for at least three decades. Residents of the old Confederacy have the worst health outlooks of anyone in the country. The North-South inequality is still very real.

How does the Left respond to this? Generally, by blaming Southerners. As I have acknowledged throughout this essay, race and racism have had a significant impact on the South. The original commitment to slavery is responsible for the region's underdevelopment, and the failure of a sufficient number of white Southerners to seek unity across racial lines has limited the possibilities for change. However, Northern occupation and exploitation has played a role that cannot be dismissed. This is something almost no left-wing voice is willing to acknowledge today.

An example of the way this plays out in the realm of scholarship is afforded by the analytic essay sociologist Chandra Childers wrote for the Economic Policy Institute in 2024, titled "The Evolution of the Southern Economic Development Strategy," and tellingly subtitled "rooted in racism." Childers recognizes that the South is distinctly lacking in state protections for its working class. It is a region of low regulation, low wages, and low taxes. Each of these elements she seeks to explain by reference to the history of slavery. For example, she attributes regressive taxes, and their persistence until the present day, to the influence of the planter class and its use of "racial animus to divide poor and working-class Southerners along the lines of race." As we have seen, the planter class can hardly be said to have controlled the South consistently from the time of the Civil War to the present. Nor does this view have any place for the many Southerners who were eagerly complicit in dividing the South along lines of race but who were *also* fierce advocates of regulation, redistribution, and the rights of the (white) working class. Finally, it doesn't explain such inconvenient facts as the presence of a state income tax in Mississippi before there was one in New York, and before the implementation of a federal income tax (by a Southern president). This is history with history removed. It is as though nothing has changed from the heyday of slavery, as if the South has no history apart from that of its long-vanquished planter elite. It is past time that we began to normalize the history of the South, to speak of it not in terms of sin and redemption but to engage in a balanced examination of the facts. One of the most important facts to consider is that the role of the South in American history has been that of a foil for politically aggressive capitalists. These capitalists and their descendants have much more to do with the inequities and hardships of today's America than their old, ignominious Southern rivals.